Decorative
Frames and Borders

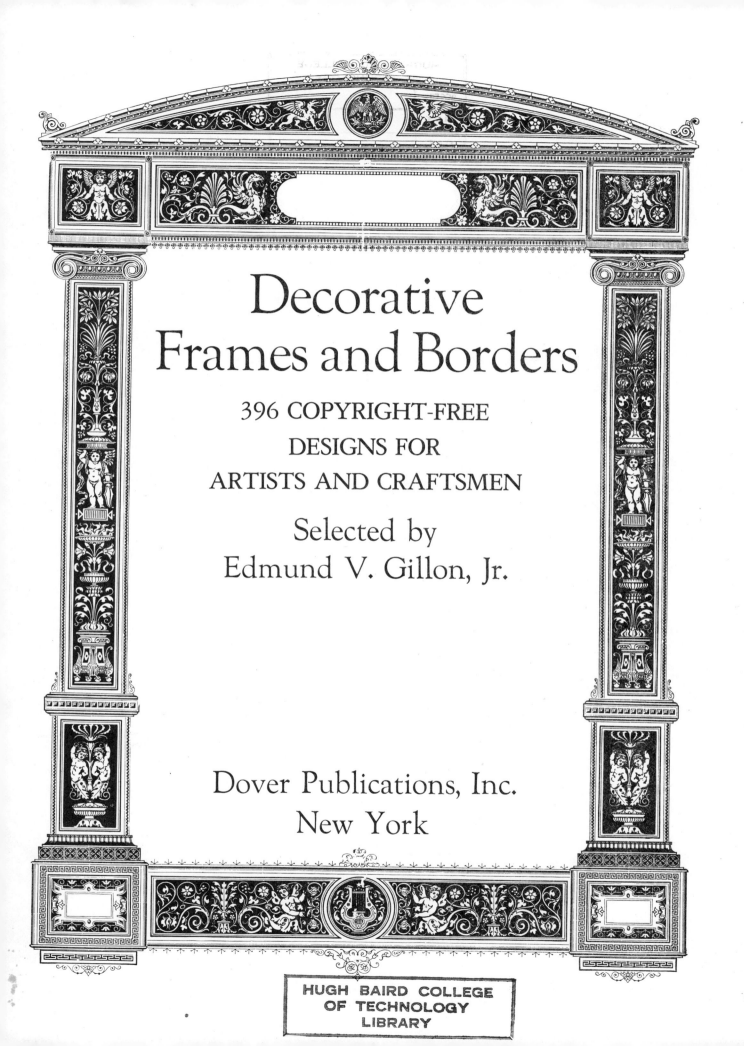

Decorative Frames and Borders

396 COPYRIGHT-FREE
DESIGNS FOR
ARTISTS AND CRAFTSMEN

Selected by
Edmund V. Gillon, Jr.

Dover Publications, Inc.
New York

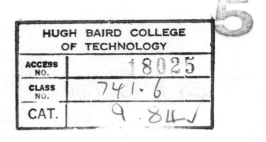
Published in Canada by General Publishing
Company, Ltd., 30 Lesmill Road, Don Mills,
Toronto, Ontario.
Published in the United Kingdom by Constable
and Company, Ltd., 10 Orange Street, London WC 2.

*Decorative Frames and Borders: 396 Copyright-
Free Designs for Artists and Craftsmen* is a new
work, first published by Dover Publications, Inc., in
1973. The illustrations were selected from a number
of different sources, as listed in the Index of
Sources. The publisher wishes to thank Cheney
Brothers for the use of several of their illustrations.

DOVER *Pictorial Archive* SERIES

This volume belongs to the Dover Pictorial
Archive Series; up to ten illustrations may be reproduced on any one project or in any single
publication, free and without special permission.
Wherever possible, include a credit line indicating
the title of this book, author and publisher. Please
address the publisher for permission to make more
extensive use of illustrations in this book than that
authorized above.

The reproduction of this book in whole is
prohibited.

International Standard Book Number: 0-486-22928-9
Library of Congress Catalog Card Number: 72-96186

Manufactured in the United States of America
Dover Publications, Inc.
180 Varick Street
New York, N. Y. 10014

Publisher's Note.

Working from the basic idea of a four-sided or round enclosure, the human imagination has produced an endless variety of border designs. This volume is perhaps the largest and most varied collection of borders and frames ever compiled, including every style, mood and form as interpreted through the whole range of art movements and historical periods. And yet, we have only surveyed the field; the simple rectangular frame is capable of infinite elaboration.

Many of these designs were originally used in books, on title pages, text pages and illustrations. Others were found on tradesmen's cards, advertisements and announcements, menus and certificates. Such decorations have come in and out of style and are now enjoying a renewed popularity in modern forms of graphics—book covers, posters and packagings. Of course, their use today need not be related to their original purpose; what was once a utilitarian commercial ornament, for example, might serve a more purely esthetic function in a collage. Careful and imaginative choosing is the key to using this randomly arranged catalog.

Among the historical periods represented are the Renaissance, Baroque, Rococo, French Empire and Victorian, many of them in the form of modern reinterpretations. There are neo-Greek and Roman motifs, Persian, Egyptian, Arabesque and Pre-Raphaelite designs, as well as Art Nouveau and Art Deco. In addition to the floral, architectural and geometric forms that make up most of these designs, various miscellaneous elements find their way into borders for special purposes or occasions. These include wreaths for Christmas and black cats for Halloween, allegories of time and justice, shoes and bales and barrels representing the trades. In a McLuhanesque sense, the illustrative border is the medium which conveys the message as convincingly as any verbal matter printed within it.

Over 40 books were used in compiling this collection, all of them listed in the Index of Sources, with complete bibliographical information and the figures which were taken from each one. Specimen books issued by type foundries and typesetters catalogs, both American and European, supplied many of the illustrations. Others were drawn from anthologies of ornamental and commercial artwork. Several of the plates were reproduced directly from the original books in which they first appeared. These include an 1898 collection of nursery rhymes, with whimsical borders for each page, and an edition of Spenser's *Shepheard's Calender* illustrated by Walter Crane. Although some of the illustrations are the work of known artists and designers, such as Thomas M. Cleland and Daniel Berkeley Updike, most of them are anonymous ornaments intended to draw attention to the material which they enclosed.

Decorative
Frames and Borders

B·G·G 1902

5

9

8

11

10

13

15

T. M. Cleland inv. & del.

16

18

19

21

24

23

H.
SIMMONDS
W.

25

27

29

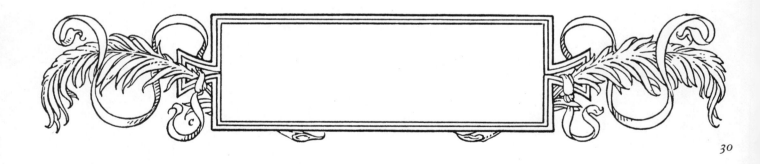

30

31

33

34

35

36 a

36 b

T. M. Cleland   inv. &del.

37

25

26

39

41

40

42

31

46

45

48

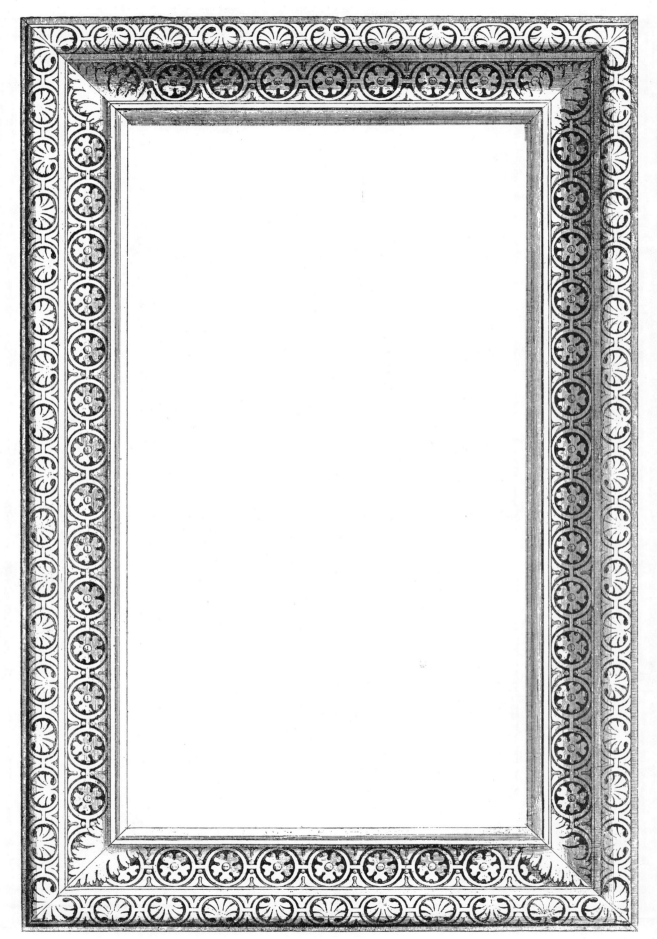

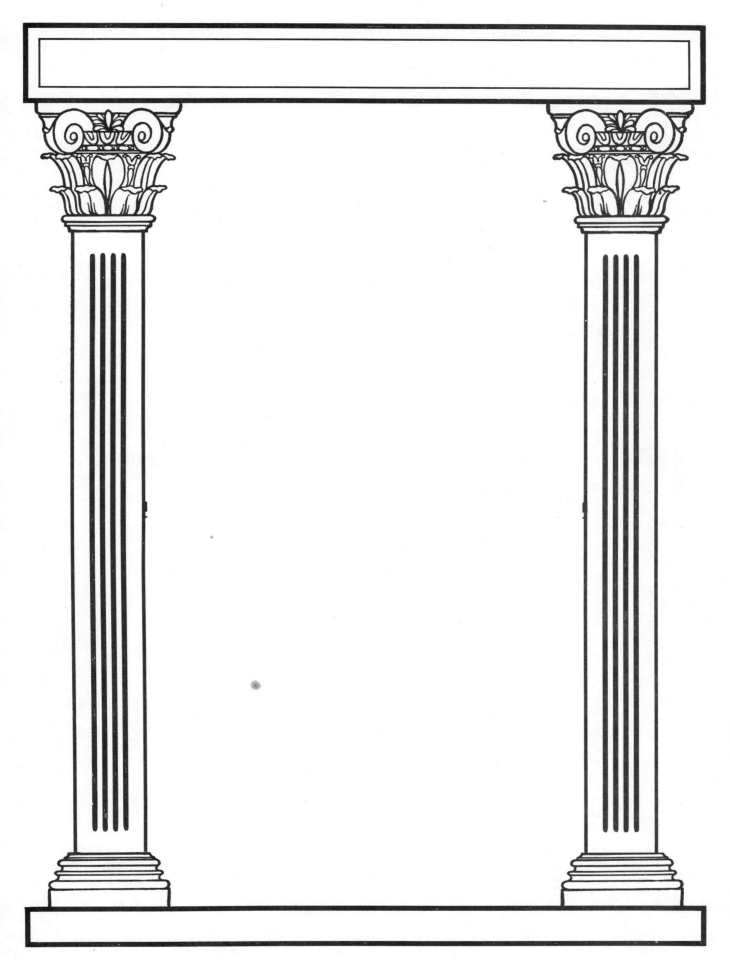

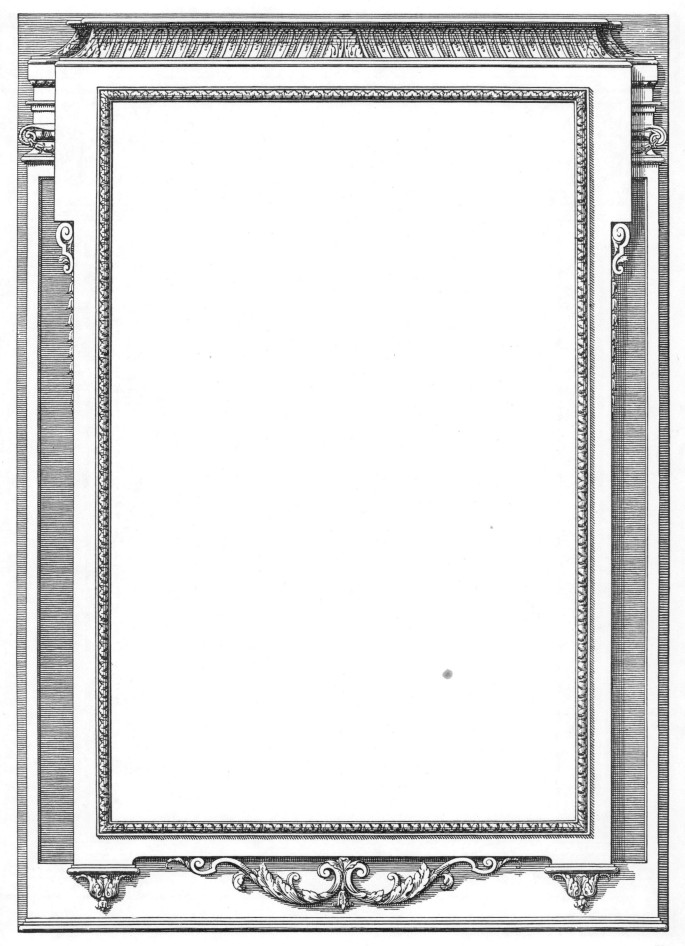

51

55

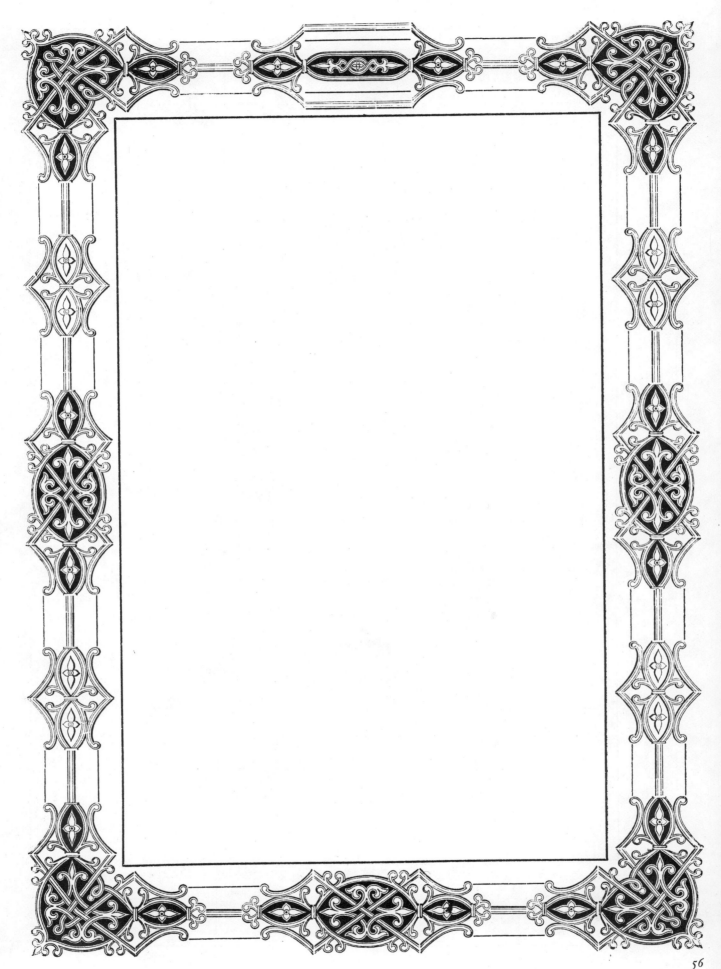

41

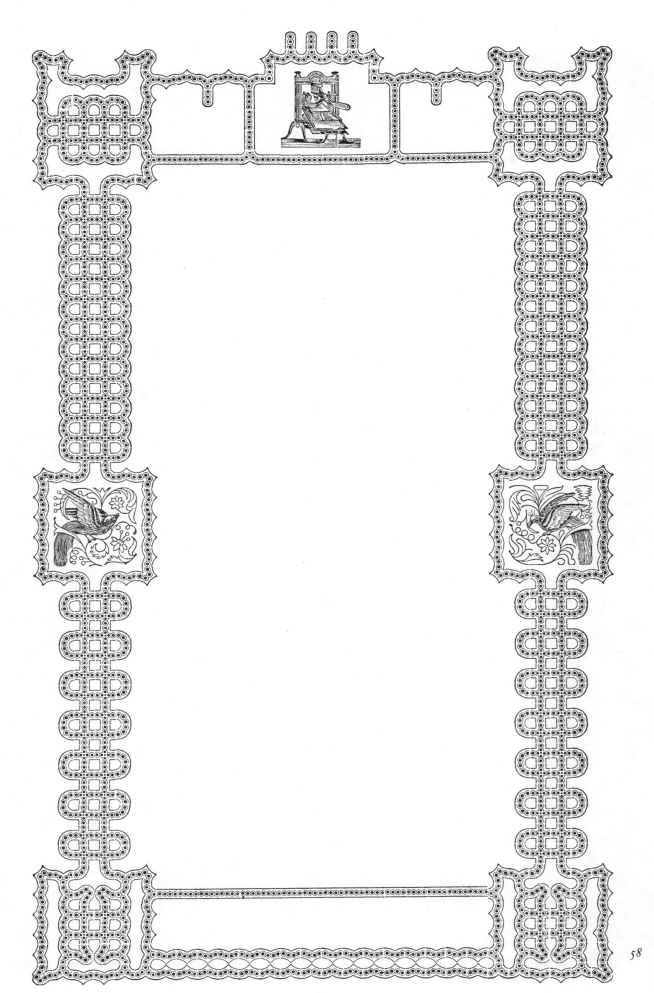

58

59

61

62

45

63

64

65

46

66

67

47

68

48

69

70

50

71

72

73

51

74

52

75

53

76

77

78

79

80

81

82

83

84

85

86

87

88

89

90

91

92

93

94

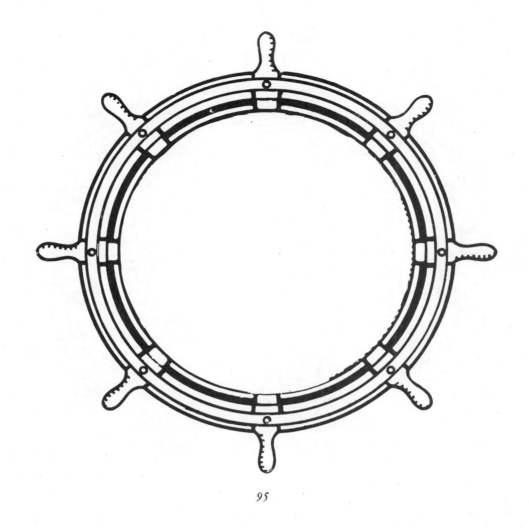

95

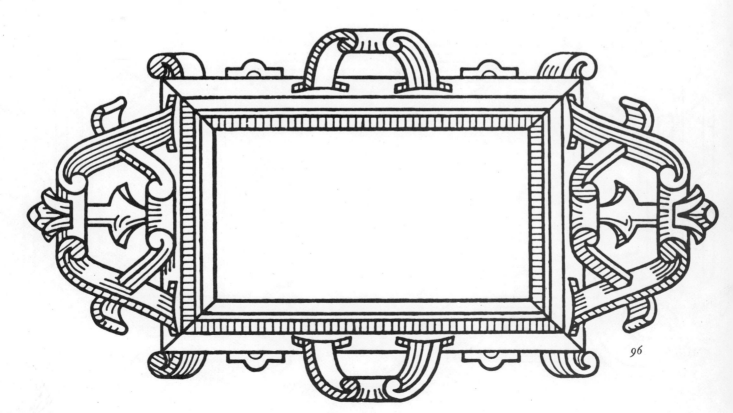

96

97

98

DEBERNY

63

100

102

101

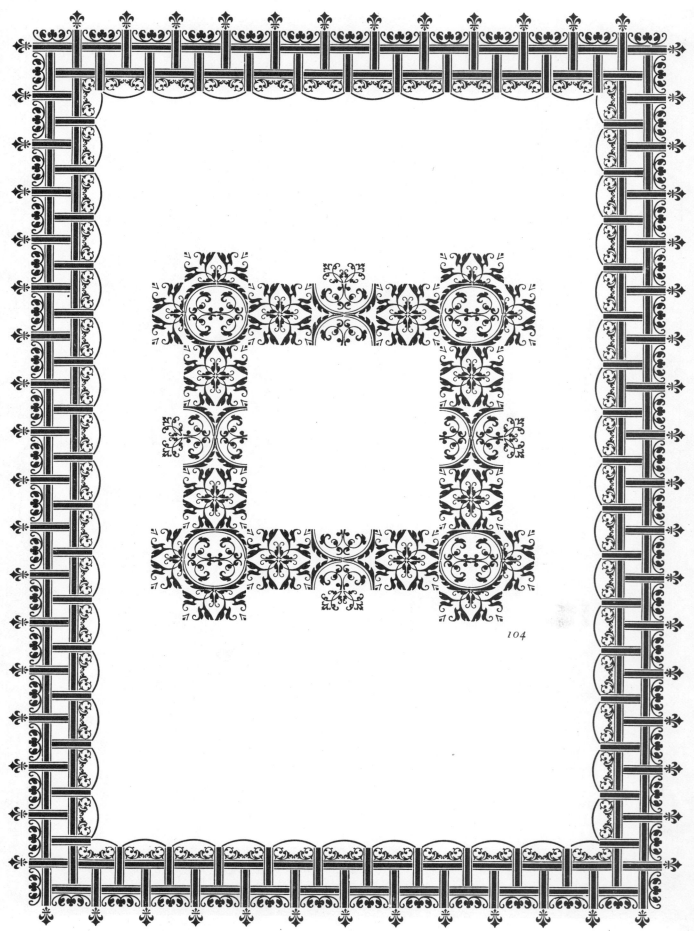

104

103

106

105

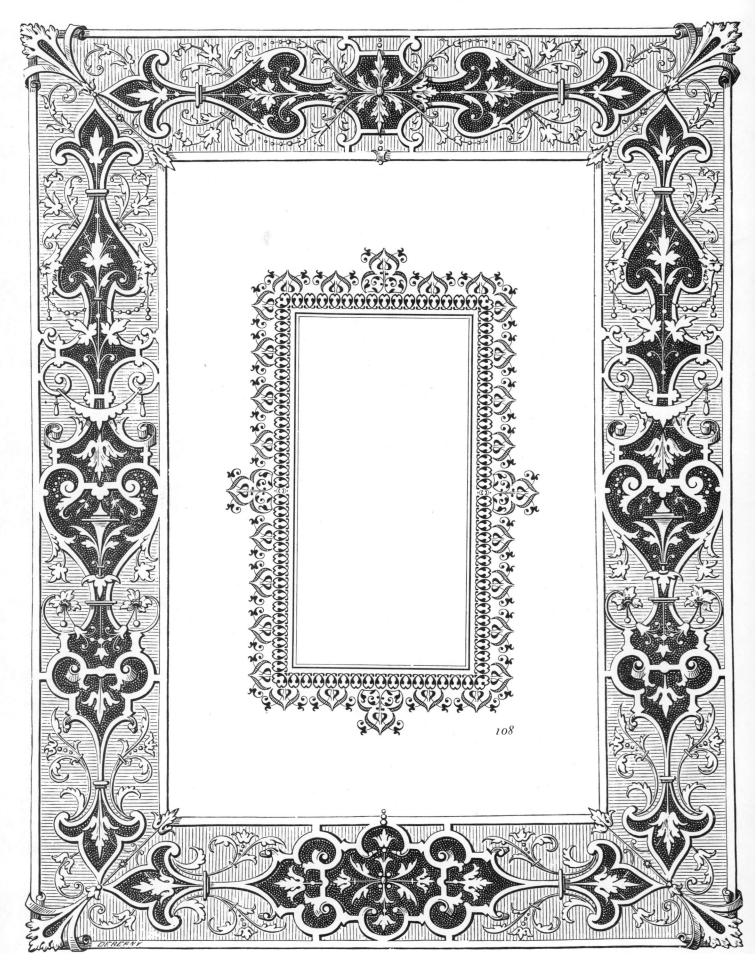

108

107

110

109

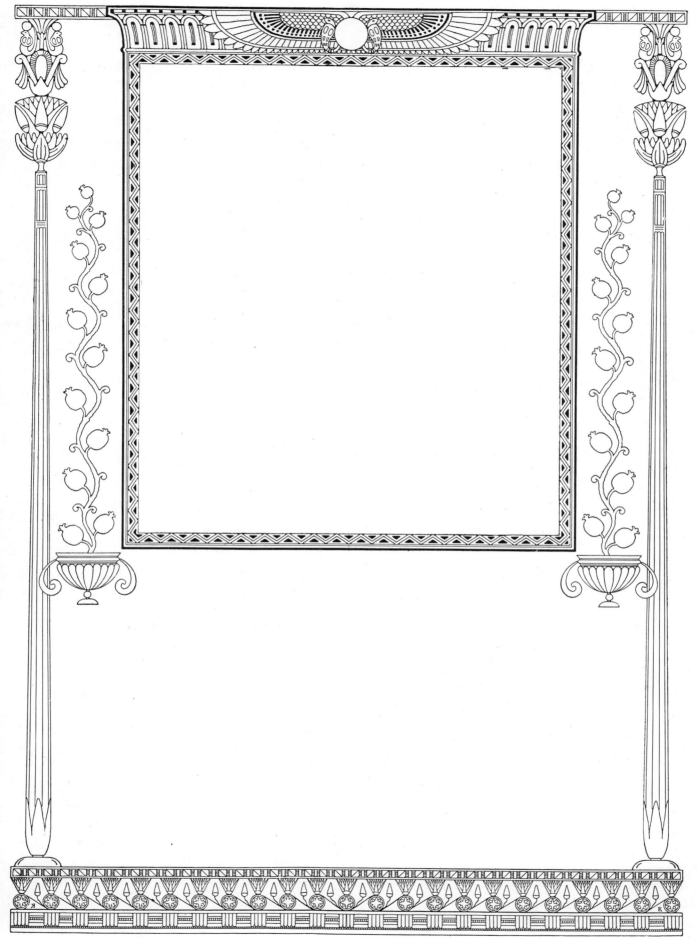

71

BK

113

114

115

QUESNEL

A. GIRALDON
04

116

118

117

119

120

121

122

123

124

125

126

128

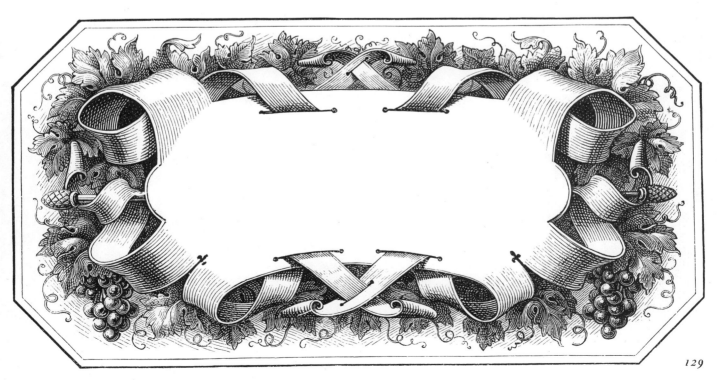

129

132

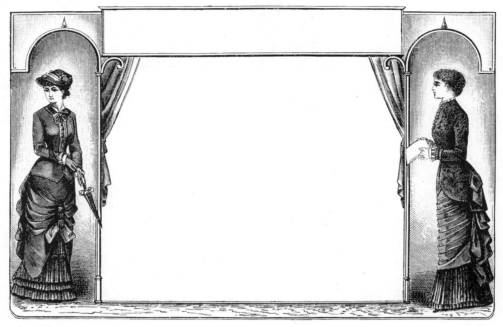

133

134

135

136

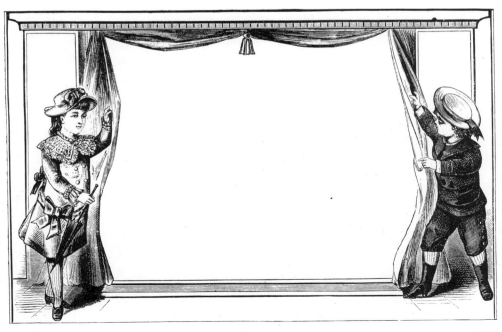

137

138

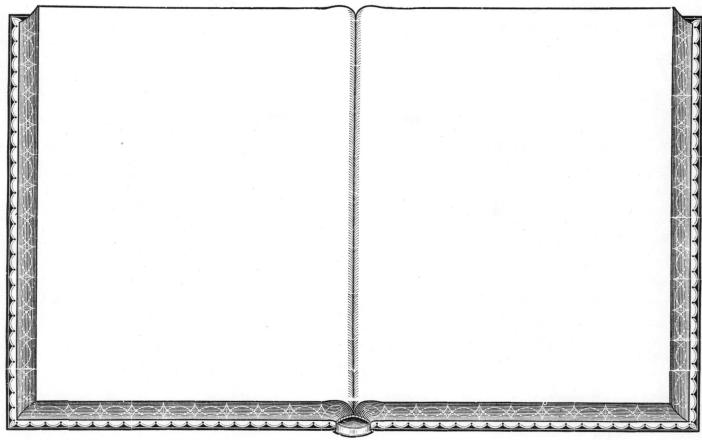

139

140

141

143

144

145

147

148

DEBERNY

150

149

151

152

153

155

154

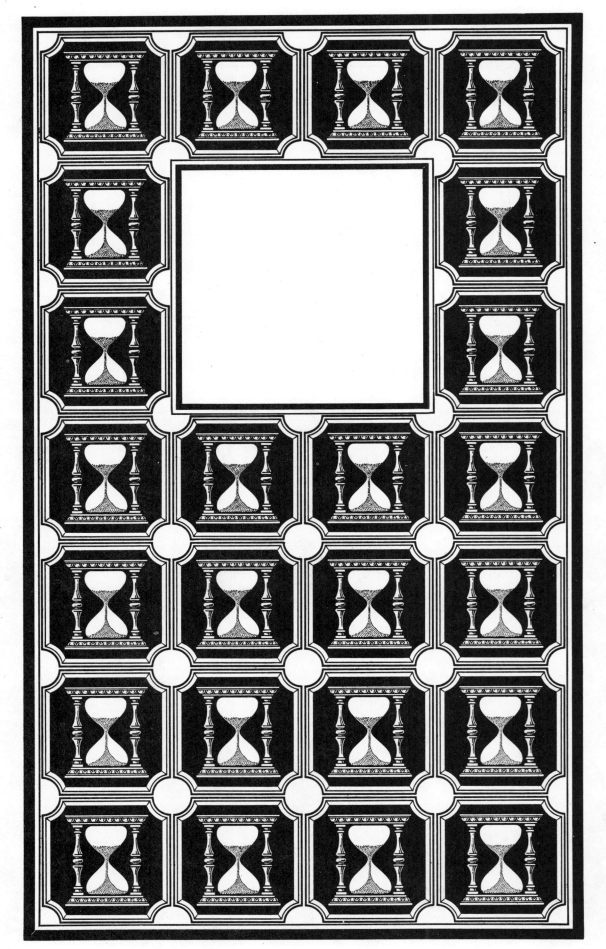

157

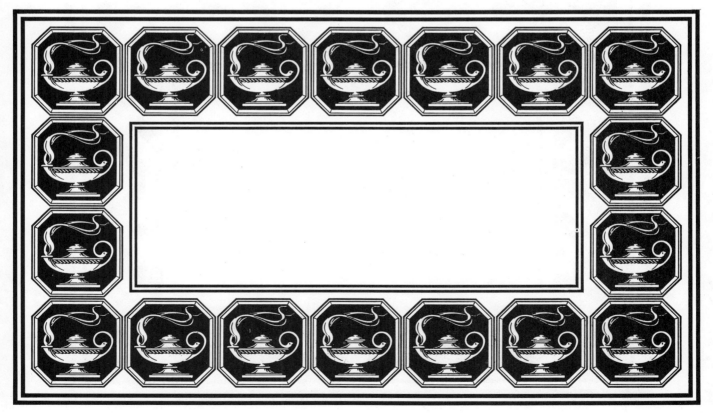

158

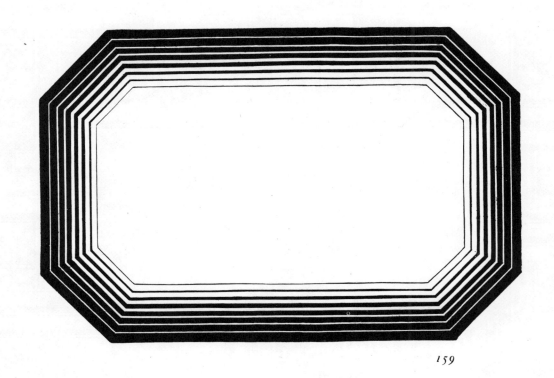

159

160

96

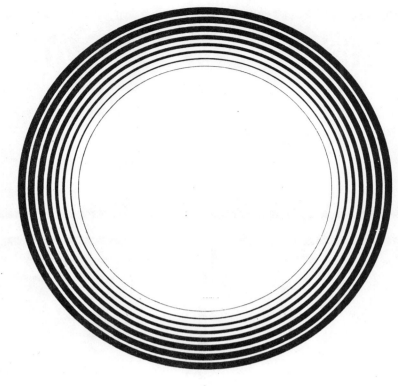

162

163

164

165

100

167

168

169

170

171

101

172

173

174

176

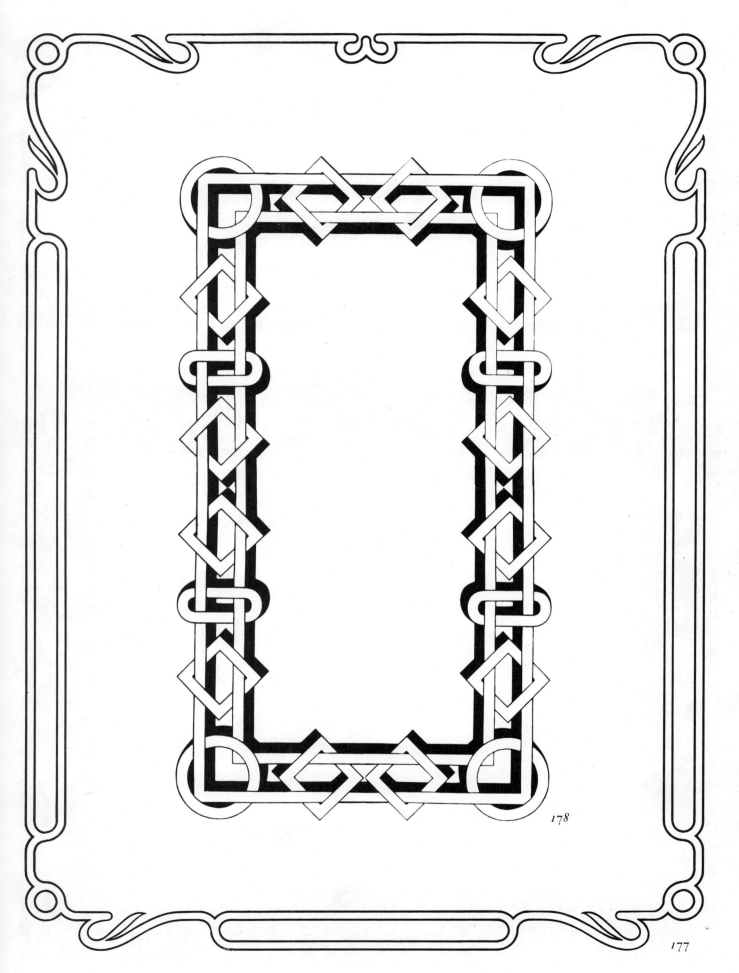

178

177

179

180

181

182

183

184

185

186

187

188

189

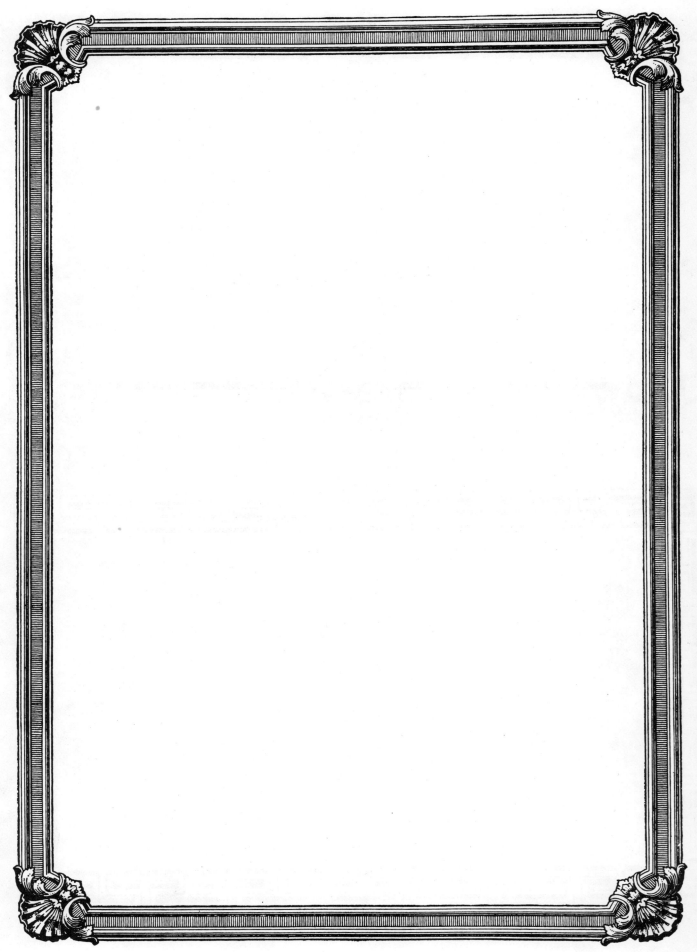

191

192

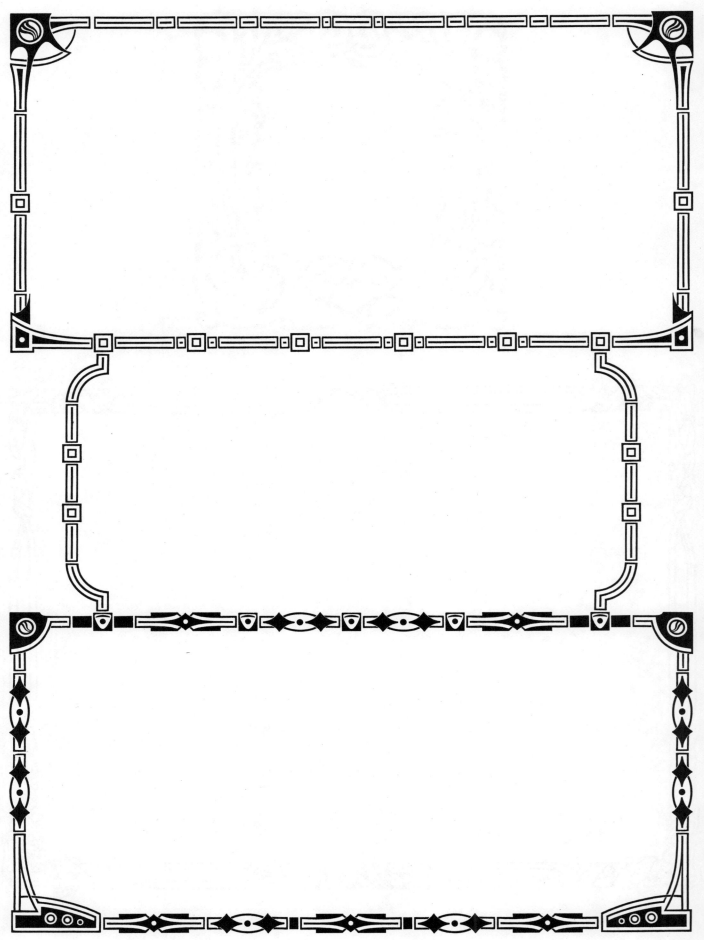

193

194

195

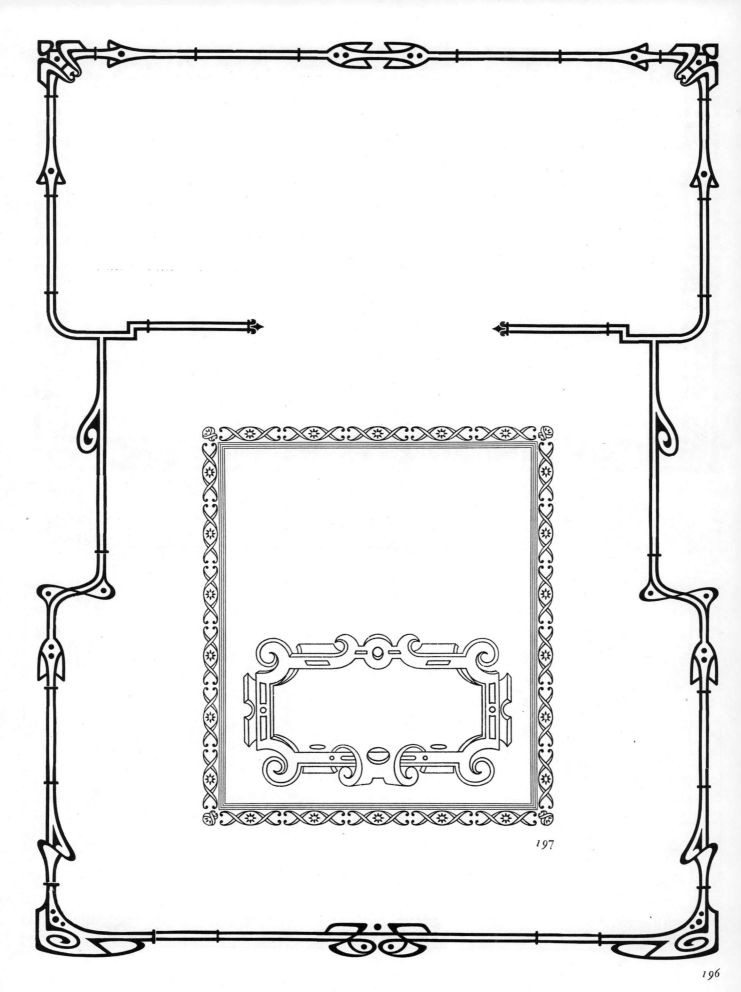

197

196

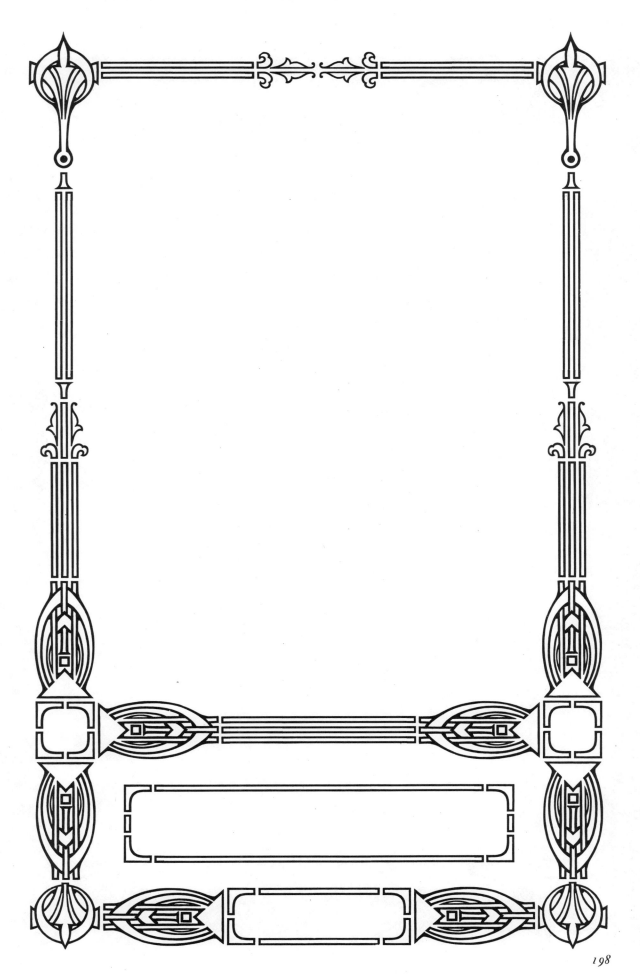

198

201

202

205

206

207

208

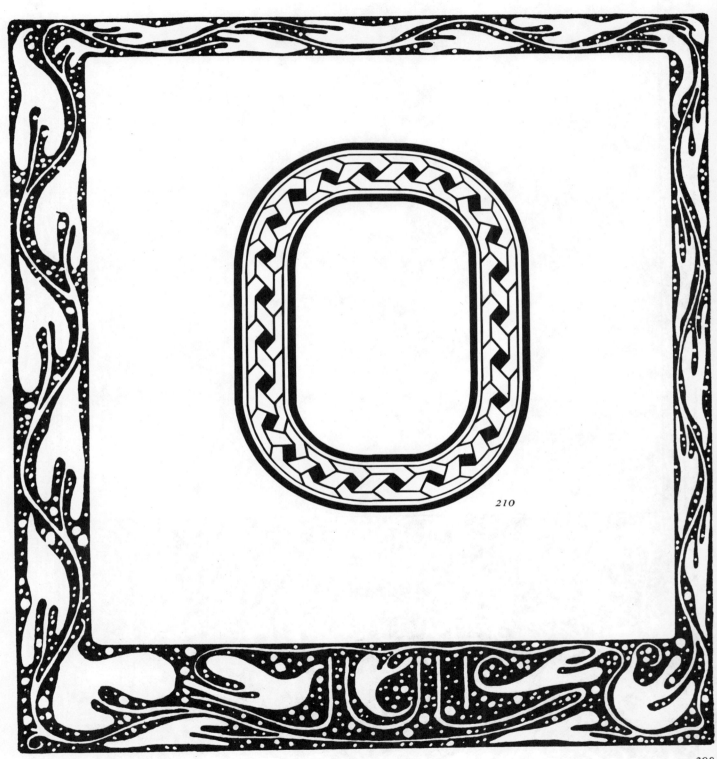

210

209

126

J. B.

211

212

214

213

215

218

219

221

220

222

223

225

224

226

227

228

229

230

231

232

233

234

235

237

236

239

238

240

241

242

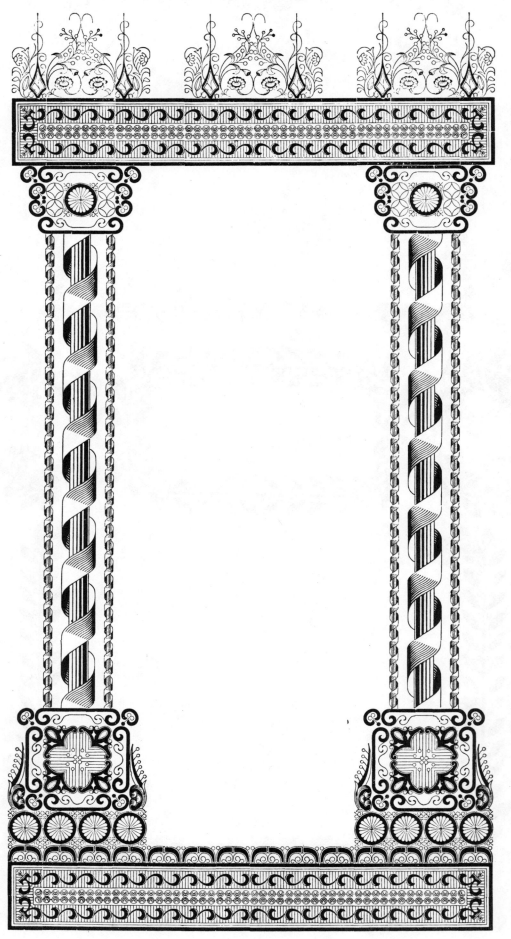

142

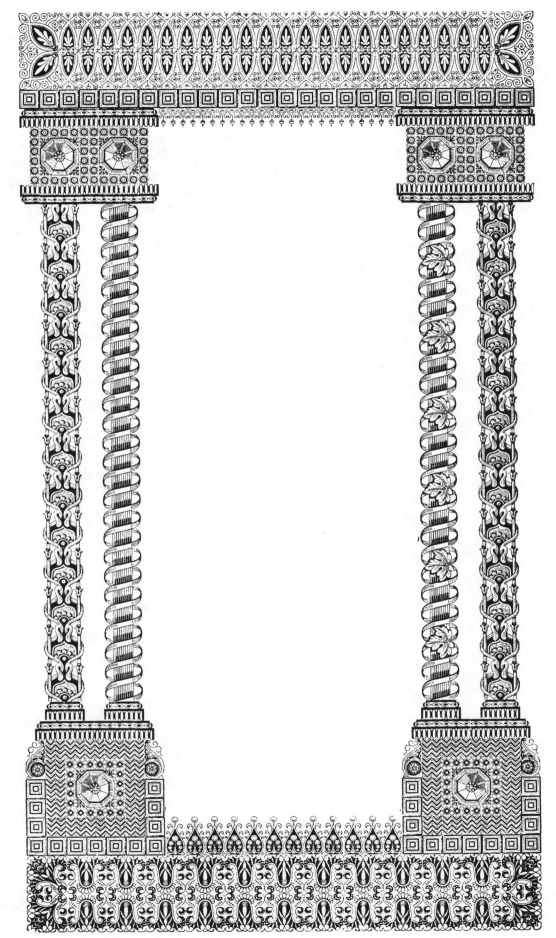

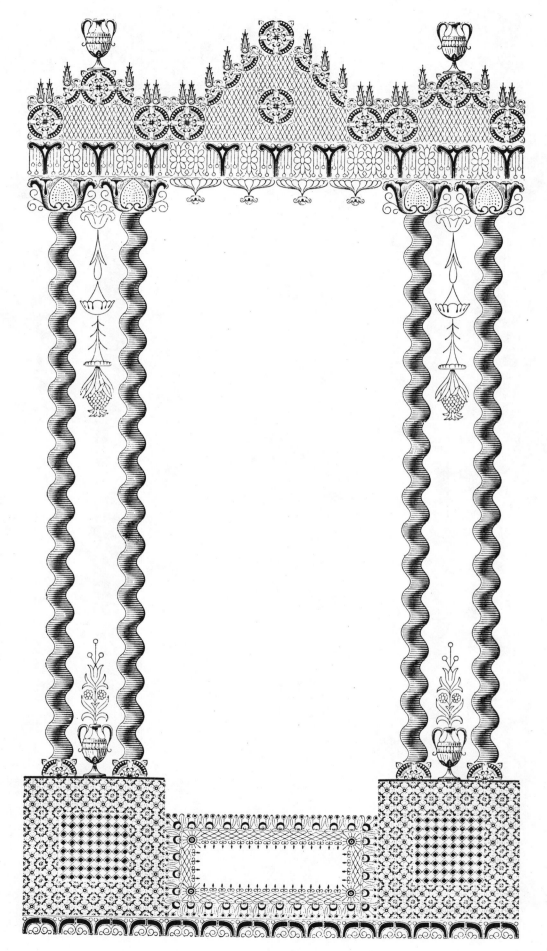

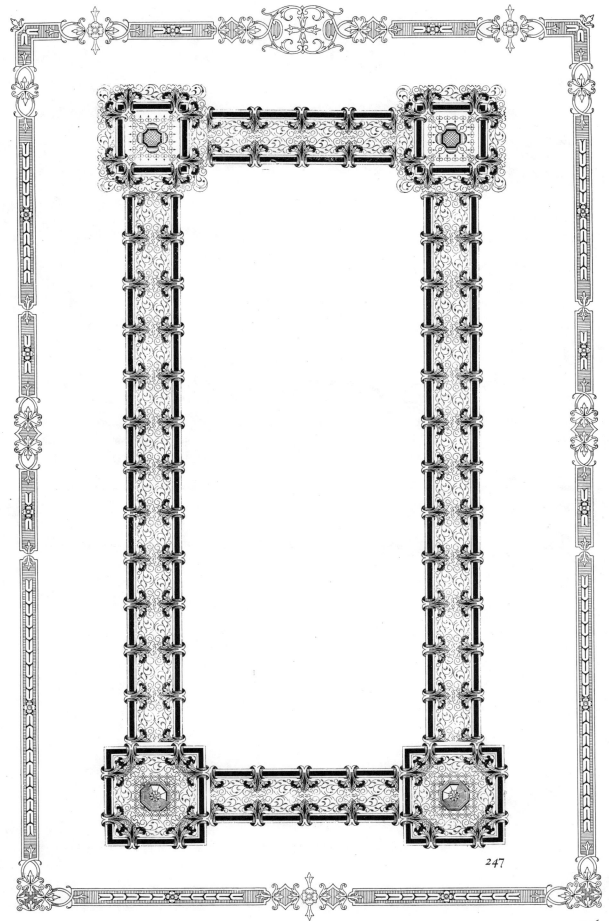

247

246

248

249

251

250

252

253

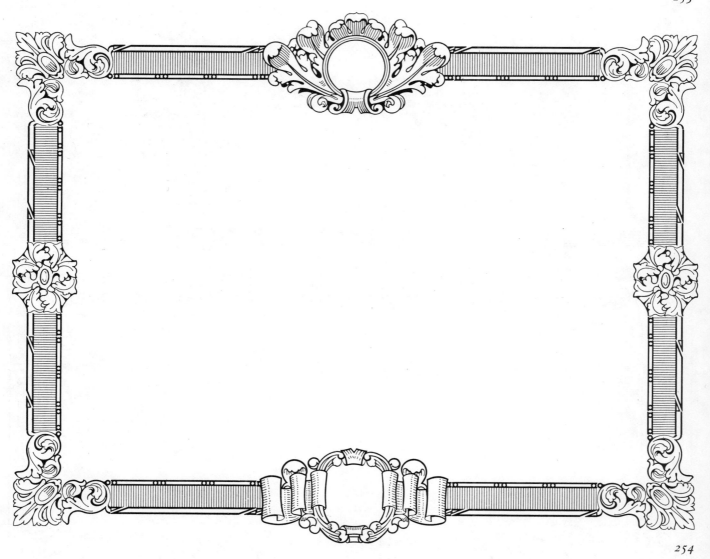

254

148

255

256

257

259

258

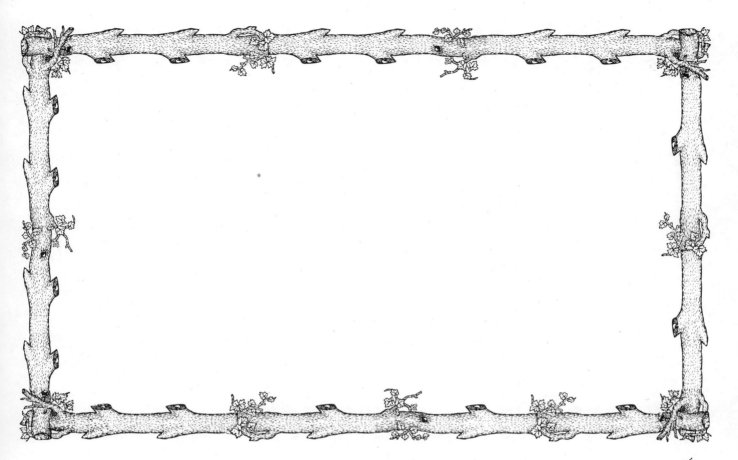

260

261

262

263

264

265

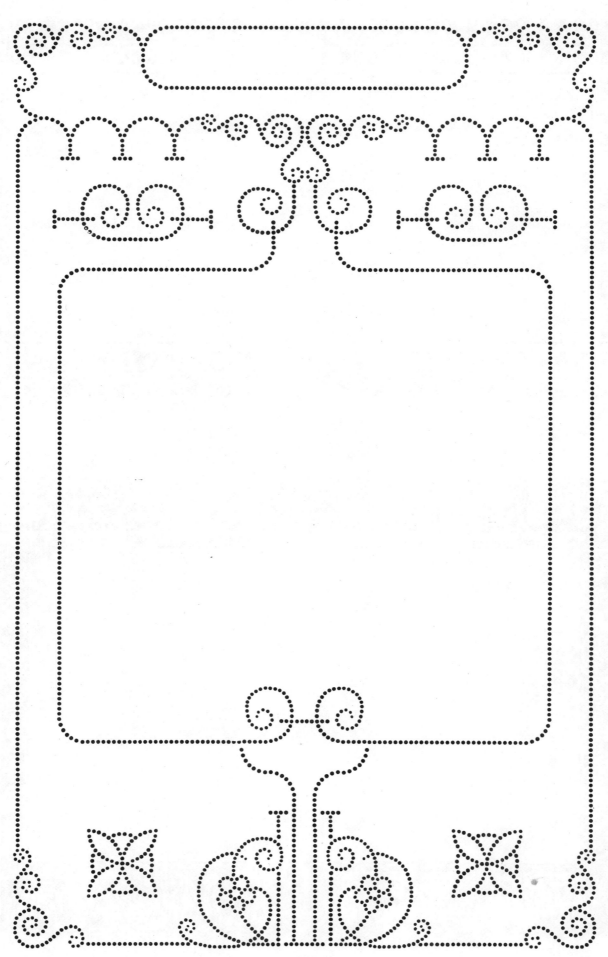

154

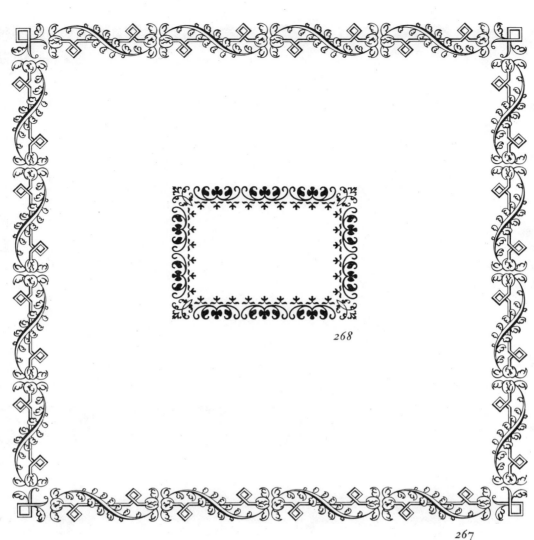

268

267

269

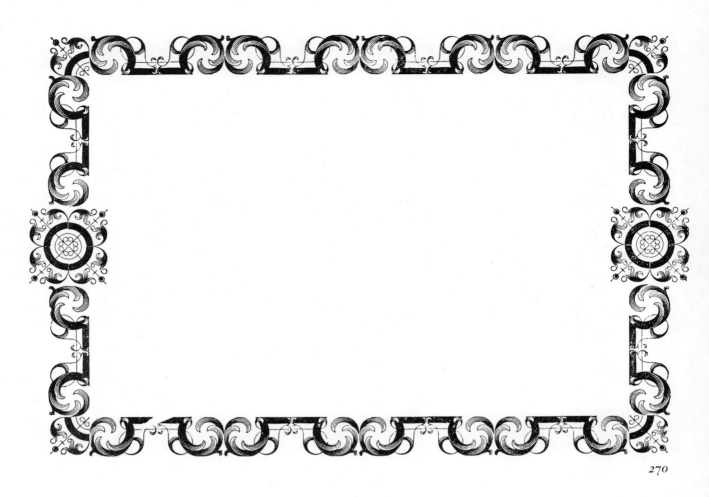

270

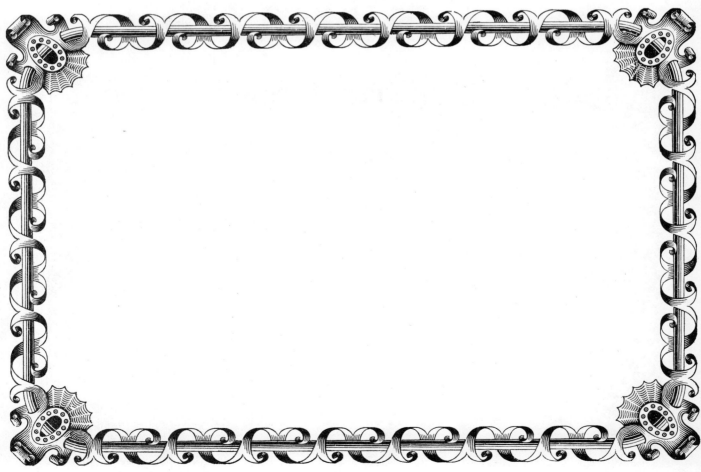

271

272

273

275

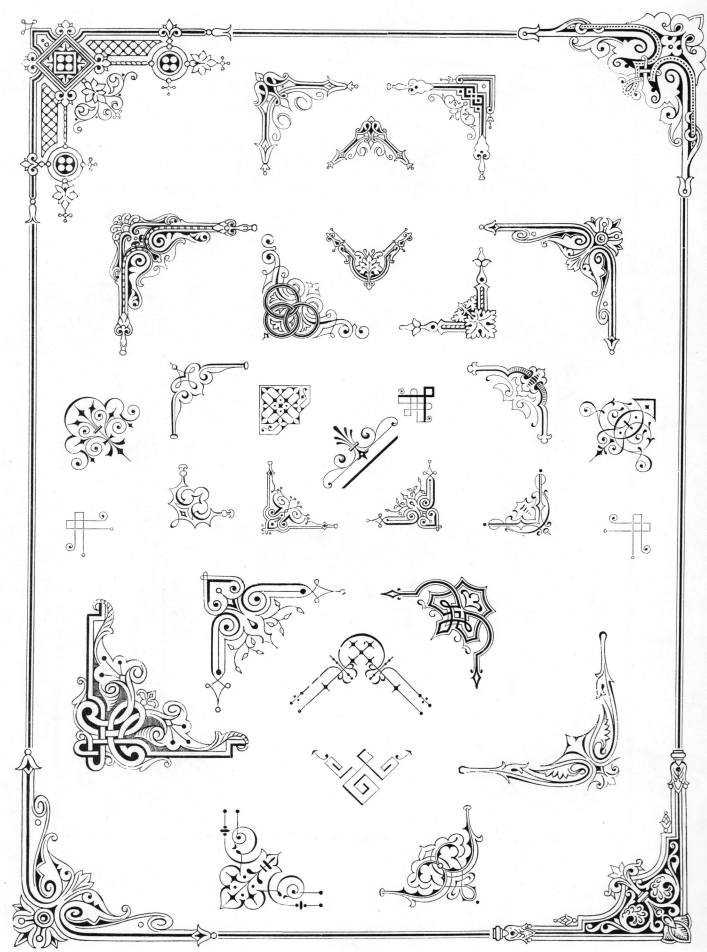

277a

161

277b

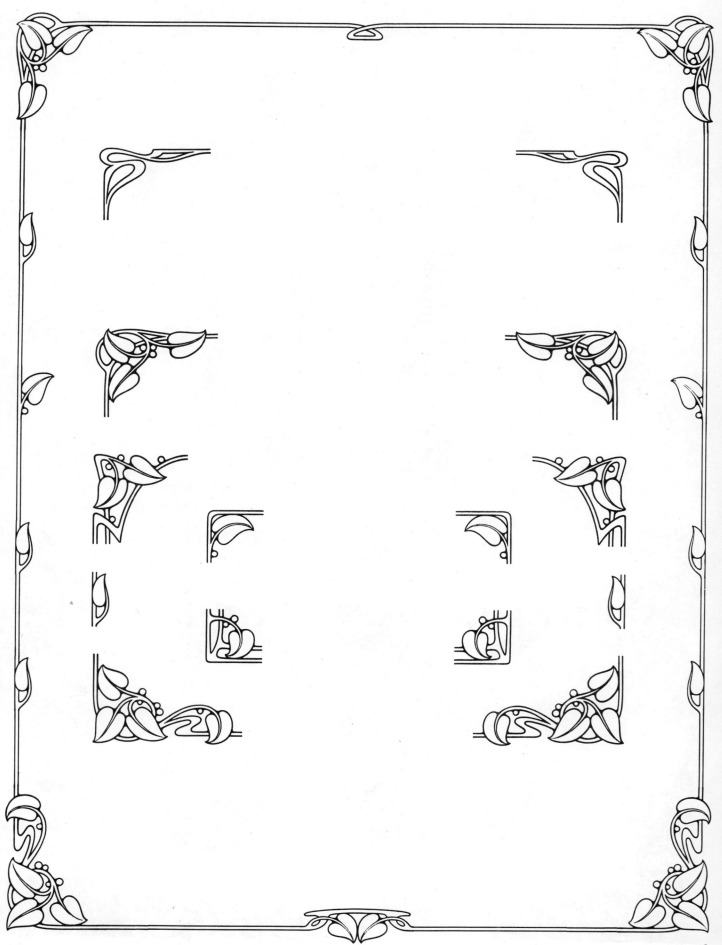

279

163

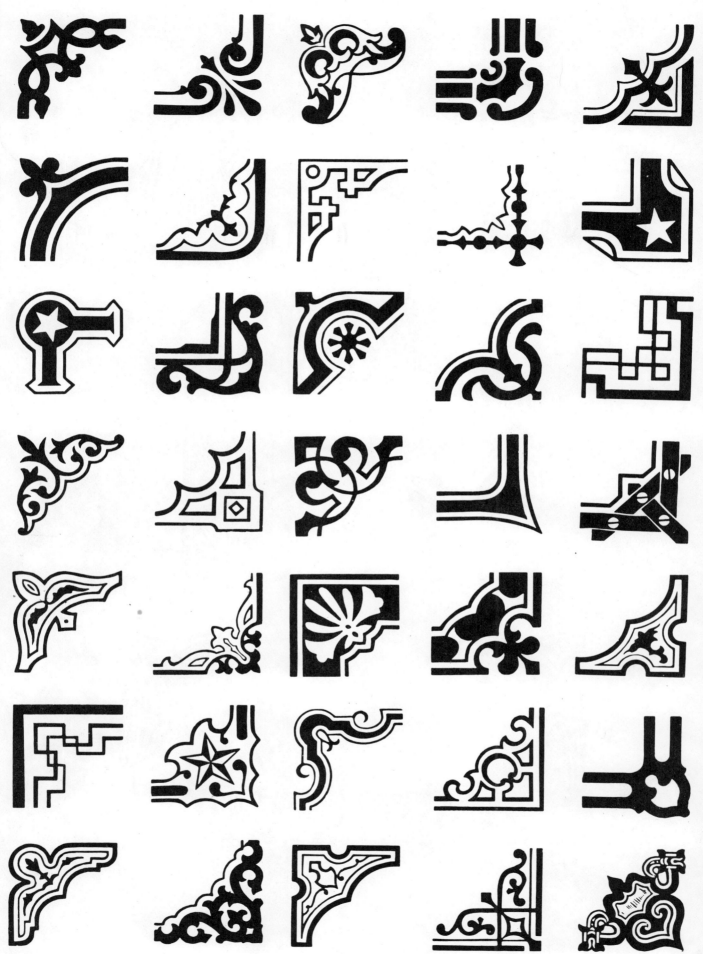

281a

281b

281c

282a

282 b

282c

282d

282e

282f

282g

282h

282i

166

283a

283b

283c

283d

283e

283f

283g

167

284a

284b

284c

284d

284e

284f

William Morris

284g

285a

285b

285c

285d

285e

285f

285g

285h

285i

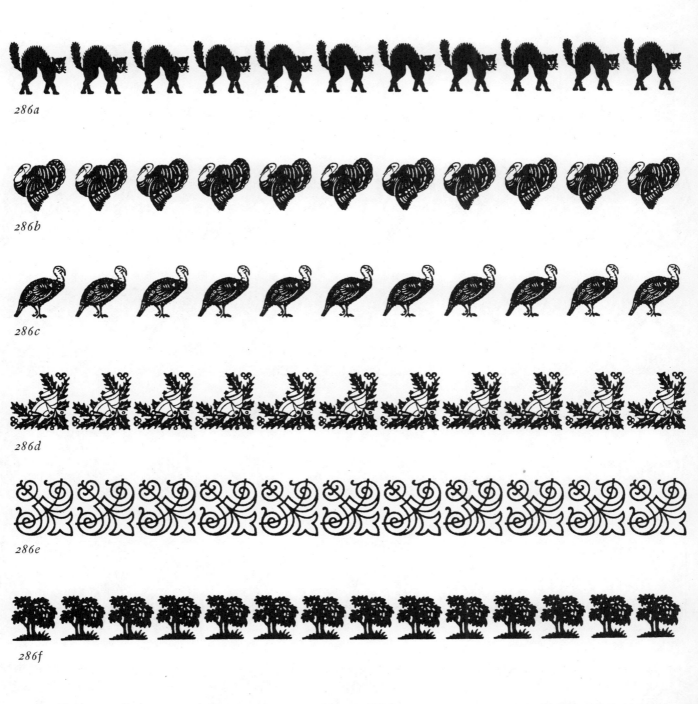

286a

286b

286c

286d

286e

286f

286g

Index of Sources

Gress, Edmund G. *The Art and Practice of Typography: A Manual of American Printing.* (2nd. ed.). New York: Oswald Publishing Co., 1917. 9, 100, 259

Hill, Thomas E. *Hill's Manual of Social and Business Forms.* Chicago: Hill Standard Book Co., 1891. 130, 131, 139

Hlastas, Stanley C. *Printing Types and How to Use Them.* Pittsburgh: Carnegie Press, Carnegie Institute of Technology, 1950. 12

Hofstätter, Hans H. *Jugendstil Druckkunst.* Baden-Baden: Holle-Verlag, 1968. 207–209, 211, 215

Inland Type Foundry. *Specimen Book and Catalog* (Pony Specimen Book). St. Louis: 1907. 232

Keystone Type Foundry. *Specimen Book of Type.* Philadelphia: 1899. 102, 230, 260, 280

Klinkhardt, Julius. *Gesamt-Probe der Schriftgiesserei Julius Klinkhardt in Leipzig und Wien.* Leipzig und Wien: 1883. 67, 80, 84, 123, 124, 129, 133–135, 137, 141, 143, 155, 159, 162

L'Art Pour Tous: Encyclopédie de L'art Industriel et Décoratif. Paris: A. Morel, Libraire-Éditeur, 1868. 49, 78, 92, 222

Lanston Monotype Corporation Limited. *A Book of "Monotype" Ornaments.* 59, 103–106, 108, 109, 146, 213, 248, 249, 251, 264, 268

Ludlow Typograph Company. *Ludlow Borders and Ornaments.* Chicago. 265, 282a, b, d, e, f, h, 283a, d, e, g, 284a, b, g

MacKellar, Smiths, and Jordan Foundry. *11th Book of Specimens of Printing Types.* Philadelphia: 1892. 56, 110, 114, 121, 127, 187, 188, 214

Museum der Modernen Kunstindustrie. *Muster-Sammlung von Hervorragenden Gegenständen der Letzten Weltausstellungen von London und Paris: Ein Handbuch von Vorlagen für Industrielle Aller Zweige.* Leipzig, Berlin und Wien: F. A. Brockhaus, 1873. 68–77

The New Colophon, II, Part 5 (Jan., 1949). 46

Orcutt, William Dana, and Bartlett, Edward E. *The Manual of Linotype Typography.* Brooklyn, N. Y.: Mergenthaler Linotype Co., 1923. 190, 285g–i

Plomer, Henry R. *English Printers' Ornaments.* London: Grafton & Co., 1924. 2, 273, 284f

Poortenaar, Jan. *The Art of the Book and Its Illustration.* London: George G. Harrap & Co. Ltd., 1935. 263

Raguenet. *Materiaux et Documents.* Vol 3. Paris: Librairie R. Ducher. 49, 61

Rosenfeld, Morris. *Lieder des Ghetto.* Berlin: S. Calvary & Co. 203–206, 216

INDEX OF SOURCES

Schriftgiesserei Ludwig and Mayer. *Kleine Schriftprobe*. Frankfurt a/M.   26, 117, 276, 277a, 282c, 284c, d

Specimens and Price List of Wood Letter.   176

Spenser, Edmund. *The Shepheard's Calender*. Illustrated by Walter Crane. London and New York: Harper & Brothers, 1898.   201, 202

Trueman, Thomas. *The Nurse's Rhyme Book: A New Collection of Nursery Rhymes, Games, Stories and Jingles*. Philadelphia: J. & J. L. Gihon, 1847.   147, 262, 269–271

Updike, Daniel Berkeley. *Updike: American Printer and His Merrymount Press*. New York: The American Institute of Graphic Arts, 1947.   41

Warren, Garnet, and Cheney, Horace B. *The Romance of Design*. New York: Doubleday, Page & Co., 1926. The publisher wishes to thank Cheney Brothers for the use of these designs.   40, 42, 111–113

White, John T. *John T. White's Specimen*. New York.   20, 58, 99, 125, 126

Zeese, A., and Company. *Specimens of Electrotypes Comprising Cuts, Borders, Ornaments, Etc.* Chicago: 1885.   128, 142, 144, 145

The following figures are from unknown sources: 5, 23, 24, 56, 58–60, 62, 64, 65, 79, 81, 85–91, 97, 98, 107, 116, 118, 120, 122, 132, 136, 138, 140, 150, 151, 178, 186, 210, 219, 238–240, 242–245

Dover Books on Art

Dover Books on Art

PRINCIPLES OF ART HISTORY, H. Wölfflin. This remarkably instructive work demonstrates the tremendous change in artistic conception from the 14th to the 18th centuries, by analyzing 164 works by Botticelli, Dürer, Hobbema, Holbein, Hals, Titian, Rembrandt, Vermeer, etc., and pointing out exactly what is meant by "baroque," "classic," "primitive," "picturesque," and other basic terms of art history and criticism. "A remarkable lesson in the art of seeing," SAT. REV. OF LITERATURE. Translated from the 7th German edition. 150 illus. 254pp. 6⅛ x 9¼.   20276-3 Paperbound $4.50

FOUNDATIONS OF MODERN ART, A. Ozenfant. Stimulating discussion of human creativity from paleolithic cave painting to modern painting, architecture, decorative arts. Fully illustrated with works of Gris, Lipchitz, Léger, Picasso, primitive, modern artifacts, architecture, industrial art, much more. 226 illustrations. 368pp. 6⅛ x 9¼.   20215-1 Paperbound $6.95

METALWORK AND ENAMELLING, H. Maryon. Probably the best book ever written on the subject. Tells everything necessary for the home manufacture of jewelry, rings, ear pendants, bowls, etc. Covers materials, tools, soldering, filigree, setting stones, raising patterns, repoussé work, damascening, niello, cloisonné, polishing, assaying, casting, and dozens of other techniques. The best substitute for apprenticeship to a master metalworker. 363 photos and figures. 374pp. 5½ x 8½.
                                                   22702-2 Paperbound $5.00

SHAKER FURNITURE, E. D. and F. Andrews. The most illuminating study of Shaker furniture ever written. Covers chronology, craftsmanship, houses, shops, etc. Includes over 200 photographs of chairs, tables, clocks, beds, benches, etc. "Mr. & Mrs. Andrews know all there is to know about Shaker furniture," Mark Van Doren, NATION. 48 full-page plates. 192pp. 7⅞ x 10¾.   20679-3 Paperbound $5.00

LETTERING AND ALPHABETS, J. A. Cavanagh. An unabridged reissue of "Lettering," containing the full discussion, analysis, illustration of 89 basic hand lettering styles based on Caslon, Bodoni, Gothic, many other types. Hundreds of technical hints on construction, strokes, pens, brushes, etc. 89 alphabets, 72 lettered specimens, which may be reproduced permission-free. 121pp. 9¾ x 8.   20053-1 Paperbound $3.50

THE HUMAN FIGURE IN MOTION, Eadweard Muybridge. The largest collection in print of Muybridge's famous high-speed action photos. 4789 photographs in more than 500 action-strip-sequences (at shutter speeds up to 1/6000th of a second) illustrate men, women, children—mostly undraped—performing such actions as walking, running, getting up, lying down, carrying objects, throwing, etc. "An unparalleled dictionary of action for all artists," AMERICAN ARTIST. 390 full-page plates, with 4789 photographs. Heavy glossy stock, reinforced binding with headbands. 7⅞ x 10¾.   20204-6 Clothbound $15.95

Dover Books on Art

GREEK REVIVAL ARCHITECTURE IN AMERICA, T. Hamlin. A comprehensive study of the American Classical Revival, its regional variations, reasons for its success and eventual decline. Profusely illustrated, displaying the work of almost every important architect. 2 appendices. 39 figures, 94 plates containing 221 photos, 62 architectural designs, drawings, etc. 324-item classified bibliography. Index. xi + 439pp. 5⅜ x 8½.

21148-7 Paperbound $7.50

CREATIVE LITHOGRAPHY AND HOW TO DO IT, Grant Arnold. Written by a man who practiced and taught lithography for many years, this highly useful volume explains all the steps of the lithographic process from tracing the drawings on the stone to printing the lithograph, with helpful hints for solving special problems. Index. 16 reproductions of lithographs. 11 drawings. xv + 214pp. of text. 5⅜ x 8½.

21208-4 Paperbound $4.50

ARABIC ART IN COLOR, Prisse d'Avennes. 50 full-color plates from rare 19th-century volumes by noted French historian. 141 authentic Islamic designs and motifs from Cairo art treasures include florals, geometrics, Koran illuminations, spots, borders, etc. Ranging from 12th to 18th century, these exquisite illustrations will interest artists, designers of textiles and wallpaper, craftspeople working in stained glass, rugs, etc. Captions. 46pp. 9⅜ x 12¼.

23658-7 Paperbound $6.00

DESIGN AND EXPRESSION IN THE VISUAL ARTS, J. F. A. Taylor. Here is a much needed discussion of art theory which relates the new and sometimes bewildering directions of 20th century art to the great traditions of the past. The first discussion of principle that addresses itself to the eye rather than to the intellect, using illustrations from Rembrandt, Leonardo, Mondrian, El Greco, etc. List of plates. Index. 59 reproductions. 5 color plates. 75 figures. x + 245pp. 5⅜ x 8½.

21195-9 Paperbound $4.00

THE ALPHABET AND ELEMENTS OF LETTERING, F. W. Goudy. A beautifully illustrated volume on the aesthetics of letters and type faces and their history and development. Each plate consists of 15 forms of a single letter with the last plate devoted to the ampersand and the numerals. 27 full-page plates. 48 additional figures. xii + 131pp. 7⅞ x 10¾.

20792-7 Paperbound $4.00

THE COMPLETE BOOK OF SILK SCREEN PRINTING PRODUCTION, J. I. Biegeleisen. Here is a clear and complete picture of every aspect of silk screen technique and press operation—from individually operated manual presses to modern automatic ones. Unsurpassed as a guidebook for setting up shop, making shop operation more efficient, finding out about latest methods and equipment; or as a textbook for use in teaching, studying, or learning all aspects of the profession. 124 figures. Index. Bibliography. List of Supply Sources. xi + 253pp. 5⅜ x 8½.

21100-2 Paperbound $4.00

Dover Books on Art

MASTERPIECES OF FURNITURE, Verna Cook Salomonsky. Photographs and measured drawings of some of the finest examples of Colonial American, 17th century English, Windsor, Sheraton, Hepplewhite, Chippendale, Louis XIV, Queen Anne, and various other furniture styles. The textual matter includes information on traditions, characteristics, background, etc. of various pieces. 101 plates. Bibliography. 224pp. 7⅞ x 10¾.

21381-1 Paperbound $6.00

PRIMITIVE ART, Franz Boas. In this exhaustive volume, a great American anthropologist analyzes all the fundamental traits of primitive art, covering the formal element in art, representative art, symbolism, style, literature, music, and the dance. Illustrations of Indian embroidery, paleolithic paintings, woven blankets, wing and tail designs, totem poles, cutlery, earthenware, baskets and many other primitive objects and motifs. Over 900 illustrations. 376pp. 5⅜ x 8.   20025-6 Paperbound $5.00

AN INTRODUCTION TO A HISTORY OF WOODCUT, A. M. Hind. Nearly all of this authoritative 2-volume set is devoted to the 15th century—the period during which the woodcut came of age as an important art form. It is the most complete compendium of information on this period, the artists who contributed to it, and their technical and artistic accomplishments. Profusely illustrated with cuts by 15th century masters, and later works for comparative purposes. 484 illustrations. 5 indexes. Total of xi + 838pp. 5⅜ x 8½. Two-vols. 20952-0,20953-0 Paperbound $13.00

A HISTORY OF ENGRAVING AND ETCHING, A. M. Hind. Beginning with the anonymous masters of .15th century engraving, this highly regarded and thorough survey carries you through Italy, Holland, and Germany to the great engravers and beginnings of etching in the 16th century, through the portrait engravers, master etchers, practicioners of mezzotint, crayon manner and stipple, aquatint, color prints, to modern etching in the period just prior to World War I. Beautifully illustrated —sharp clear prints on heavy opaque paper. Author's preface. 3 appendixes. 111 illustrations. xviii + 487 pp. 5⅜ x 8½.

20954-7 Paperbound $7.50

ART STUDENTS' ANATOMY, E. J. Farris. Teaching anatomy by using chiefly living objects for illustration, this study has enjoyed long popularity and success in art courses and home-study programs. All the basic elements of the human anatomy are illustrated in minute detail, diagrammed and pictured as they pass through common movements and actions. 158 drawings, photographs, and roentgenograms. Glossary of anatomical terms. x + 159pp. 5⅝ x 8⅜.   20744-7 Paperbound $3.50

COLONIAL LIGHTING, A. H. Hayward. The only book to cover the fascinating story of lamps and other lighting devices in America. Beginning with rush light holders used by the early settlers, it ranges through the elaborate chandeliers of the Federal period, illustrating 647 lamps. Of great value to antique collectors, designers, and historians of arts and crafts. Revised and enlarged by James R. Marsh. xxxi + 198pp. 5⅝ x 8¼.

20975-X Paperbound $4.50

Dover Books on Art

VITRUVIUS: TEN BOOKS ON ARCHITECTURE. The most influential book in the history of architecture. 1st century A.D. Roman classic has influenced such men as Bramante, Palladio, Michelangelo, up to present. Classic principles of design, harmony, etc. Fascinating reading. Definitive English translation by Professor H. Morgan, Harvard. 344pp. 5⅜ x 8.

20645-9 Paperbound **$5.00**

HAWTHORNE ON PAINTING. Vivid re-creation, from students' notes, of instructions by Charles Hawthorne at Cape Cod School of Art. Essays, epigrammatic comments on color, form, seeing, techniques, etc. "Excellent," Time. 100pp. 5⅜ x 8.

20653-X Paperbound **$2.25**

THE HANDBOOK OF PLANT AND FLORAL ORNAMENT, R. G. Hatton. 1200 line illustrations, from medieval, Renaissance herbals, of flowering or fruiting plants: garden flowers, wild flowers, medicinal plants, poisons, industrial plants, etc. A unique compilation that probably could not be matched in any library in the world. Formerly "The Craftsman's Plant-Book." Also full text on uses, history as ornament, etc. 548pp. 6⅛ x 9¼.

20649-1 Paperbound **$7.95**

DECORATIVE ALPHABETS AND INITIALS, Alexander Nesbitt. 91 complete alphabets, over 3900 ornamental initials, from Middle Ages, Renaissance printing, baroque, rococo, and modern sources. Individual items copyright free, for use in commercial art, crafts, design, packaging, etc. 123 full-page plates. 3924 initials. 129pp. 7¾ x 10¾.

20544-4 Paperbound **$5.00**

METHODS AND MATERIALS OF THE GREAT SCHOOLS AND MASTERS, Sir Charles Eastlake. (Formerly titled "Materials for a History of Oil Painting.") Vast, authentic reconstruction of secret techniques of the masters, recreated from ancient manuscripts, contemporary accounts, analysis of paintings, etc. Oils, fresco, tempera, varnishes, encaustics. Both Flemish and Italian schools, also British and French. One of great works for art historians, critics; inexhaustible mine of suggestions, information for practicing artists. Total of 1025pp. 5⅜ x 8.

20718-8, 20719-6 Two volume set, Paperbound **$15.00**

AMERICAN VICTORIAN ARCHITECTURE, edited by Arnold Lewis and Keith Morgan. Collection of brilliant photographs of 1870's, 1880's, showing finest domestic, public architecture; many buildings now gone. Landmark work, French in origin; first European appreciation of American work. Modern notes, introduction. 120 plates. "Architects and students of architecture will find this book invaluable for its first-hand depiction of the state of the art during a very formative period," ANTIQUE MONTHLY. 152pp. 9 x 12.

23177-1 Paperbound **$7.95**

THE HUMAN FIGURE, J. H. Vanderpoel. Not just a picture book, but a complete course by a famous figure artist. Extensive text, illustrated by 430 pencil and charcoal drawings of both male and female anatomy. 2nd enlarged edition. Foreword. 430 illus. 143pp. 6⅛ x 9¼.

20432-4 Paperbound **$3.00**

Dover Books on Art

THE FOUR BOOKS OF ARCHITECTURE, Andrea Palladio. A compendium of the art of Andrea Palladio, one of the most celebrated architects of the Renaissance, including 250 magnificently-engraved plates showing edifices either of Palladio's design or reconstructed (in these drawings) by him from classical ruins and contemporary accounts. 257 plates. xxiv + 119pp. 9½ x 12¾.   21308-0 Paperbound $10.00

150 MASTERPIECES OF DRAWING, A. Toney. Selected by a gifted artist and teacher, these are some of the finest drawings produced by Western artists from the early 15th to the end of the 18th centuries. Excellent reproductions of drawings by Rembrandt, Bruegel, Raphael, Watteau, and other familiar masters, as well as works by lesser known but brilliant artists. 150 plates. xviii + 150pp. 5⅜ x 11¼.   21032-4 Paperbound $6.00

MORE DRAWINGS BY HEINRICH KLEY. Another collection of the graphic, vivid sketches of Heinrich Kley, one of the most diabolically talented cartoonists of our century. The sketches take in every aspect of human life: nothing is too sacred for him to ridicule, no one too eminent for him to satirize. 158 drawings you will not easily forget. iv + 104pp. 7⅜ x 10¾.
20041-8   Paperbound $3.75

THE HUMAN FIGURE IN MOTION, Eadweard Muybridge. The largest collection in print of Muybridge's famous high-speed action photos. 4789 photographs in more than 500 action-strip-sequences (at shutter speeds up to 1/6000th of a second) illustrate men, women, children—mostly undraped—performing such actions as walking, running, getting up, lying down, carrying objects, throwing, etc. "An unparalleled dictionary of action for all artists," AMERICAN ARTIST. 390 full-page plates, with 4789 photographs. Heavy glossy stock, reinforced binding with headbands. 7⅞ x 10¾.   20204-6 Clothbound $15.95

PAINTING IN ISLAM, Sir Thomas W. Arnold. This scholarly study puts Islamic painting in its social and religious context and examines its relation to Islamic civilization in general. 65 full-page plates illustrate the text and give outstanding examples of Islamic art. 4 appendices. Index of mss. referred to. General Index. xxiv + 159pp. 6⅝ x 9¼.   21310-2   Paperbound $6.00

THE MATERIALS AND TECHNIQUES OF MEDIEVAL PAINTING, D. V. Thompson. An invaluable study of carriers and grounds, binding media, pigments, metals used in painting, al fresco and al secco techniques, burnishing, etc. used by the medieval masters. Preface by Bernard Berenson. 239pp. 5⅜ x 8.
20327-1   Paperbound $3.50

THE HISTORY AND TECHNIQUE OF LETTERING, A. Nesbitt. A thorough history of lettering from the ancient Egyptians to the present, and a 65-page course in lettering for artists. Every major development in lettering history is illustrated by a complete aphabet. Fully analyzes such masters as Caslon, Koch, Garamont, Jenson, and many more. 89 alphabets, 165 other specimens. 317pp. 7½ x 10½.   20427-8   Paperbound $5.50

Dover Books on Art

DESIGN AND FIGURE CARVING, E. J. Tangerman. "Anyone who can peel a potato can carve," states the author, and in this unusual book he shows you how, covering every stage in detail from very simple exercises working up to museum-quality pieces. Terrific aid for hobbyists, arts and crafts counselors, teachers, those who wish to make reproductions for the commercial market. Appendix: How to Enlarge a Design. Brief bibliography. Index. 1298 figures. x + 289pp. 5⅜ x 8½.

21209-2   Paperbound $4.50

THE STANDARD BOOK OF QUILT MAKING AND COLLECTING, M. Ickis. Even if you are a beginner, you will soon find yourself quilting like an expert, by following these clearly drawn patterns, photographs, and step-by-step instructions. Learn how to plan the quilt, to select the pattern to harmonize with the design and color of the room, to choose materials. Over 40 full-size patterns. Index. 483 illustrations. One color plate. xi + 276pp. 6¾ x 9½.   20582-7   Paperbound $4.95

A HISTORY OF COSTUME, Carl Köhler. The most reliable and authentic account of the development of dress from ancient times through the 19th century. Based on actual pieces of clothing that have survived, using paintings, statues and other reproductions only where originals no longer exist. Hundreds of illustrations, including detailed patterns for many articles. Highly useful for theatre and movie directors, fashion designers, illustrators, teachers. Edited and augmented by Emma von Sichart. Translated by Alexander K. Dallas. 594 illustrations. 464pp. 5⅛ x 7⅛.

21030-8   Paperbound $6.50

Dover publishes books on commercial art, art history, crafts, design, art classics; also books on music, literature, science, mathematics, puzzles and entertainments, chess, engineering, biology, philosophy, psychology, languages, history, and other fields. For free circulars write to Dept. DA, Dover Publications, Inc., 180 Varick St., New York, N.Y. 10014.